THE WORLD AT WAR
WORLD WAR II

Children During Wartime

Heinemann Library
Chicago, Illinois

. . . . Brenda Williams

Editorial: Andrew Farrow and Dan Nunn
Design: Lucy Owen and Tokay Interactive Ltd
 (www.tokay.co.uk)
Picture Research: Hannah Taylor and Sally
 Claxton
Production: Duncan Gilbert

Originated by Repro Multi Warna
Printed and bound in China by Leo Paper Group

10
10 9 8 7 6 5 4 3 2

**Library of Congress Cataloging-in-
Publication Data**
Williams, Brenda, 1946-
 Children during wartime / Brenda Williams.
  p. cm. -- (World at war-- World War II)
 Includes bibliographical references and index.
 ISBN 1-4034-6193-7 (library binding-hardcover)
 1. World War, 1939-1945--Children.
 2. Children and war.
 3. War victims.
 I. Title. II. Series.
 D810.C4W52 2005
 940.53'161--dc22
                                2005014762
 ISBN 13:978-1-4034-6193-3

Acknowledgments
The publishers would like to thank the following
for permission to reproduce photographs:

Corbis pp. **5** (Hulton Deutsch Collection), **7
bottom** (Lucien Aigner), **11 top** (Hulton Deutsch
Collection), **12** (Bettmann), **14** (Bettmann), **15
bottom** (Bettmann), **16**, **19 bottom** (Bettmann),
19 top (Bettmann), **21**, **23** (Bettmann), **24**
(Hulton Deutsch Collection), **25** (Hulton Deutsch
Collection), **27 top** (Bettmann), **27 bottom**
(Bettmann), **28** (Hulton Deutsch Collection);
Getty Images pp. **6** (Time & Life Pictures/Hugo
Jaeger), **8** (Hulton Archive), **9** (Hulton Archive),
18 (Hulton Archive), **20** (Hulton Archive);
Imperial War Museum pp. **7 top**, **10**, **26**;
Topfoto.co.uk pp. **11 bottom** (HIP/The Lord
Price Collection), **22 left** (Public Record
Office/HIP), **22 right**; Topham Picturepoint
pp. **15 top**, **17**; TRH Pictures p. **4**.

Cover photograph of a child after a German air
raid on London, August 1940, reproduced with
permission of AKG Images.

Every effort has been made to contact copyright
holders of any material reproduced in this book.
Any omissions will be rectified in subsequent
printings if notice is given to the publishers.

CONTENTS

Some words are shown in bold, **like this**. You can find out what they mean by looking in the glossary.

PREPARING FOR WAR

World War II began in September 1939. For the next six years, children in many nations grew up during wartime. Millions of children lost their homes and families. Many thousands of children lost their lives.

During the 1930s, children in Europe and Asia had already experienced war. There was a bitter **civil war** in Spain. Japan attacked China, and Abyssinia (now Ethiopia, in Africa) was attacked by Italy. War hurt many children through fear, injury, homelessness, and loss of their family. Children were also victims of religious and racial **persecution**, especially in Germany. In Germany, the **Nazis** came to power and began a campaign to drive out **Jews**. In Europe and America, there was talk of a new world war.

War in Poland

On September 1, 1939, war became real for Polish children, when German armies invaded Poland. Polish soldiers fought to defend their country. But in this new war, children and other **civilians** were in as much danger as the soldiers. Many were killed as German planes dropped bombs on homes and schools and tanks smashed through villages and cities. Many children fled from their homes to become **refugees**, but there was no escape. Poland was defeated.

On September 3, 1939, families in Great Britain heard Prime Minister Neville Chamberlain's grim radio broadcast: Britain was at war with Germany. Newspapers carried the stark headline, "WAR." Movie newsreels showed armies on the move. Across Europe and in the United States, Canada, and Australia, families waited for war news.

▲ Children were among the many refugees who packed roads in their efforts to escape to safety. But by 1940, millions of children like these in Poland were living under Nazi rule.

4

September 3, 1939	April–May 1940	July–September 1940
Britain and France go to war with Germany, which has attacked Poland.	Germany invades Norway and Denmark, then the Netherlands, Belgium, and France.	With no allies left in Europe, Britain's Empire fights alone.

Eyewitness

Some children did not understand how serious the war was. Eileen Hughes, who was in school in 1939, explains:

"Before Pearl Harbor, I didn't realize how serious the war in Europe was. I think that it ... seemed very far away. It was horrible what was going on in Europe, but I don't think I realized how close it was going to hit us, until Pearl Harbor."

Preparing for war

The United States was still at peace in 1939, though most people supported Britain and its **allies**. The U.S. government began to sell war supplies to Britain and France. It also knew that a war with Japan was possible, and began to improve the U.S. defenses. The fathers of some children joined the army. Many more air force planes were flying overhead. Navy ships left port to patrol the oceans and protect shipping. And many people went to work in the war industries. At home, people began preparations for **civilian** defense, such as practicing for air raids.

Amercan children followed the war news closely. In 1940, they learned of the **Battle of Britain**. In 1941, they heard of the invasion of the Soviet Union by German armies. Then, on December 7, 1941, Japan attacked the U.S. naval base at Pearl Harbor, in Hawaii. This attack shocked all Americans and brought the United States into the war.

▶ Children in London watch an **air raid shelter** being built in 1938. People feared that a new war would bring bombing on a scale not seen before.

June 22, 1941	December 7, 1941	December 11, 1941
Germany invades the Soviet Union (USSR). Millions of Russian civilians soon find themselves behind enemy lines.	Japanese naval planes attack the U.S. naval base at Pearl Harbor. The United States declares war on December 8.	Germany and Italy declare war on the United States.

Signs of War

There was no TV or Internet in the 1930s, but children knew a lot about war preparations. Adults talked about war. Newspapers showed photos of the world's leaders holding important meetings. Movie theaters showed world news on newsreels (short films), and audiences saw Hitler making boastful speeches to large crowds in Germany. By 1940, children sat with their families around the wireless (radio) to listen to the "Fireside Chats" of President Franklin Roosevelt, or British Prime Minister Winston Churchill's words of defiance.

Most people got war news from the radio. Families also received government brochures that explained how to cope with **air raids**, the **blackout** (preventing lights from showing at night, which would help enemy bombers), and **rationing**. Children in many countries learned to put on gas masks, cover lighted windows at night with dark blackout curtains, and clean up after air raids. At school, they pinned flags on maps to show where battles were fought. They read letters from fathers, uncles, and brothers stationed in faraway places. Everyone wondered how long the war would last.

▶ Almost every child knew about Germany's leader, Adolf Hitler. Some made jokes about his little moustache and Nazi arm salute—but Hitler was no joke. Ever since 1933, when the Nazis took power in Germany, Hitler had made news. By 1940, Germany's Führer (leader) was celebrating the defeat of France. He seemed to be winning the war.

Eyewitness

Even though Americans prepared for a war with Japan, it was a great shock when it came, as Catherine White explains:

"I saw my mother and father seated on either side of the radio, their heads bent close together as they leaned into the speaker. They were crying."

◀ A mother in a gas mask holds her baby in a special baby-mask. In the United States, only people in the armed forces had gas masks. In countries like Britain, everyone had to practice poison gas drills and keep their gas masks with them at all times. Poison gas was not used as a weapon during the war.

In the News

"Always keep your gas mask with you—day and night. Learn to put it on quickly.
1. Hold your breath.
2. Put on mask wherever you are.
3. Close window."
These instructions told people what to do if the enemy dropped poison gas bombs. They come from a poster issued in 1939 by Britain's Ministry of Home Security.

▼ American students at a school in Long Island, New York, learn about the war in Europe in 1940. The United States did not join the war until the following year.

CHILDREN ON THE MOVE

In many countries families were forced from their homes by the war. They fled from the fighting and became refugees. In the United States, the government locked up many Japanese-American families because of fears they might be spies. In Great Britain, thousands of children were moved from the cities to escape the bombing.

Evacuation

The **evacuation** of children began before the war. In 1938, some governments offered to give homes to Jewish children from Germany to save them from the Nazis. Some went to the United States. Between December 1938 and September 1939, about 10,000 children went to Britain under the *Kindertransport* (child-moving) plan. Many children who left never saw their parents again.

After the outbreak of war, many British, French, and German children became **evacuees**. They were sent away from cities to the country where they would be safer.

Refugees

In May 1940, German armies rushed into France. French roads were jammed with refugees desperate to escape the shelling and bombing. Most were women, children, and old people who had fled with whatever they could carry. When the fighting stopped, most returned home to live under German occupation.

In the News

In 1938 a German official in Hamburg wrote that "Jewish children emigrating on group transports must submit documents ... certifying that they owe no taxes ..." The Nazi laws about Jews applied even to children, and Jewish families seeking to leave Germany had to hand over all their money.

▲ For Jewish children leaving Germany, countries such as the United States, Canada, Britain, and Palestine offered refuge from the Nazis. But most children had to leave their parents and friends.

8

1933-1938
Between 1933 and 1938, over 100,000 German Jews settle in the United States. Many of them are children.

September 1939
Britain begins a mass evacuation of city children to the country. Thousands also go to Australia, Canada, the United States, New Zealand, and South Africa.

May 1940
Thousands of families leave their homes as Germany invades the Netherlands, Belgium, and France.

Internment of Japanese Americans

In the United States, anti-Japanese feeling led to the imprisonment of more than 120,000 Japanese Americans living in California and other West Coast states. The government thought they might spy for, or help, Japan. In fact, almost all were loyal Americans. The families were forced to leave their jobs and homes. They were held under guard in internment camps. Some family members were separated and put into different camps. The camps were very crowded. In many the food was poor and healthcare was inadequate.

◀ The U.S. Government reacted to the Pearl Harbor attack of 1941 by passing a new law. It banned people of Japanese **ancestry** from living or working in certain areas. Most of the people sent to internment camps were U.S. citizens, but they were forced to live for up to four years behind barbed wire.

Eyewitness

California teenager Louise Ogawa (age 16) wrote from an internment camp in Arizona to a San Diego librarian, Clara Breed. Clara wrote to Japanese Americans like Louise to keep their spirits up.

"When I stop to think how the pilgrims [of 1620] started their life, similar to ours, it makes me feel grand ..." Louise told Clara. But she "wished with all my heart that I could go back to San Diego."

June-December 1941	December 1941-1942	March 1942
Millions of Russians become refugees to escape German armies invading the Soviet Union.	Japanese armies invade Malaya, Burma, Borneo, and the Philippines.	The U.S. government opens the first internment camp to hold Japanese-American families.

Life as an Evacuee

In Great Britain, many children had to leave their homes in the cities. More than 750,000 were sent away from places that might be bombed. Some went to countries such as the United States and Canada, but most were sent to Britain's countryside. Children waved goodbye to tearful mothers as their trains left the cities.

This was a new experience for the children and the families who took care of them. Some country people complained that the "townies" (many from poor families) were dirty and had no proper shoes or clean underwear. Some city children did not like the countryside. "I miss the park," wrote one seven-year-old, while another missed electric light, telling his parents "we have candles here." But others enjoyed the fields and fresh air. Some were very sad to leave when they returned to their parents.

▶ In the spring of 1940, a London policeman checks an evacuee's information tag to make sure she is put on the right train. People were sad to see children go, but hoped they would be safe out of the cities. British TV host Michael Aspel, a wartime evacuee, remembered being given candy and nuts by smiling store clerks as he and his school friends walked to the station.

Evacuees

For many British children, evacuation meant their first long train journey. More than 750,000 children without their parents were relocated in September 1939. Local people called the children "skinnies" (because many were thin) or "townies." Gradually children returned home, and by January 1944 fewer than 200,000 were still living apart from their parents.

In the News

On September 17, 1940, the passenger ship *City of Benares* was torpedoed in the Atlantic by a German submarine (called a U-boat). The *Liverpool Daily Post* newspaper reported "294 drowned in Nazi outrage." Among the many dead were 83 evacuee children on their way to Canada. The newspaper listed the names of the victims and told its readers, "a storm added to the tragedy ... as the ship was sinking." Two girls clung to an overturned lifeboat before being rescued.

▲ This picture tried to show that being away from home was fun. Most evacuees did have fun, though one boy said he missed the sink at home, because "we have to go outside to wash here."

Eyewitness

A typical evacuee from London left home with "a gas mask in a tin box ... a haversack [bag] crammed with apples and sandwiches ... brown paper parcels with more sandwiches, chocolate, spare socks ..." Like all evacuees, the child had an information tag giving his or her name, home address, school, and destination. He or she carried a small suitcase and, in the other hand, "a wad of comics."

▶ British government posters advised parents to send their children out of bombed cities to the safety of the countryside.

LEAVE THIS TO US SONNY—<u>YOU</u> OUGHT TO BE OUT OF LONDON

MINISTRY OF HEALTH EVACUATION SCHEME

11

AIR RAIDS

World War II was the first war in which large-scale air attacks destroyed cities. Cities in Europe and Japan suffered heavy bombing. For many children, air raids became part of daily, and nightly, life.

Great Britain was bombed by German planes in 1940–1941. This bombing was known as the **Blitz** (from the German *Blitzkrieg*, meaning "lightning war"). There were more attacks in 1944, this time by V-1 flying bombs and V-2 rockets. From 1942, German cities were heavily bombed by U.S. and British planes. In the Pacific, Japanese planes bombed some Australian towns, while U.S. bombers attacked Tokyo and other Japanese cities.

▶ Air raid shelters were designed to protect people from bomb blasts. This is a public shelter in New York. Although the United States prepared for air raids, neither Japan nor Germany had bombers that could fly far enough to bomb U.S. cities on the mainland.

Living with the bombs

There were fears that bombing would create mass panic, but most people just carried on with their daily lives. Children went to school, where they learned their lessons but also practiced air-raid drills. Air raids were often at night, so children had to be woken up and taken to the shelter when the **sirens** gave the alarm. In cities where there was lots of bombing, children slept in air raid shelters instead of their bedrooms. In Britain, many Londoners slept in London Tube (Underground) railway stations.

12

September 1940	1942	June–September 1944
The German Luftwaffe begins its bombing raids on London. Known as the Blitz, it reaches its climax in 1941.	Bombing of Germany begins: the U.S. Army Air Force (USAAF) bombs by day; Britain's Royal Air Force (RAF) bombs by night.	Britain is hit by German V-1 flying bombs. More than one million people move out of London.

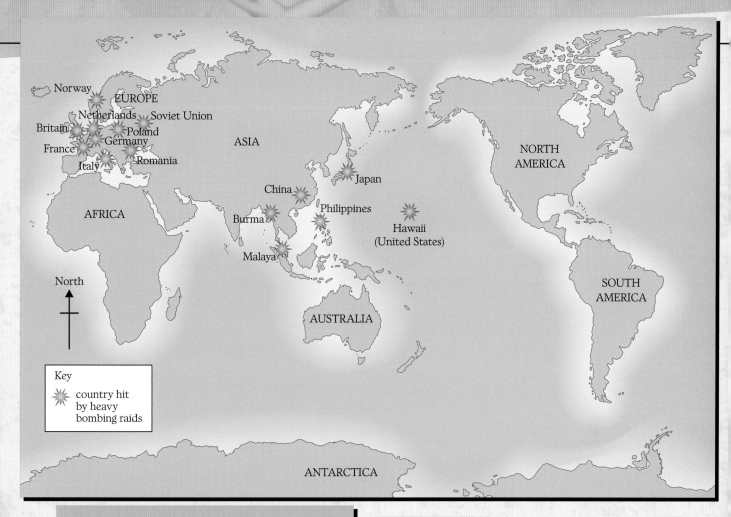

Key

⬤ country hit
by heavy
bombing raids

▲ This map shows where the heaviest
bombing raids of the war took place.

▲ This map shows where the heaviest
bombing raids of the war took place.

Raids on Germany

German children experienced the
terrors of air raids almost constantly
in 1944–1945. In Berlin, people crammed
the U-Bahn (underground/subway)
stations. With as many as 5,000 people
crowded into shelters meant for 1,500,
it was very uncomfortable. People lit
candles to determine if the air was being used up.
If a candle on the ground went out, children had to be
picked up and held at shoulder height, where there was
more oxygen. At times, the air got so bad that everyone
had to leave, even while the bombs were still falling.

Civilian bombing deaths

Australia	several hundred
Britain	over 60,000
China	over 560,000
Germany	over 600,000
Japan	over 400,000
Soviet Union	over 500,000
United States	over 200 (in Hawaii)

February 1945

Allied air raids on the
German city of Dresden kill
at least 30,000 people.

February-March 1945

American planes drop
fire-bombs on Tokyo,
Japan. More than 100,000
people are killed.

August 6 and 9, 1945

Two U.S. atomic bombs wipe out
the Japanese cities of Hiroshima
(more than 100,000 killed) and
Nagasaki (more than 40,000 killed).

What an Air Raid Was Like

Children were often in bed when night raiders flew over their homes and dropped bombs. Some children were asleep in public shelters, where people sometimes stayed at night. Other children were woken up, wrapped in coats and blankets to keep them warm, and taken to the family shelter. Some children spent the night playing games, reading, or annoying their nervous parents. Others slept right through the air raid until the "all clear" siren signal alerted people that the bombers had flown away.

After a raid, children came out into the streets to inspect the damage. They watched rescuers free people from damaged buildings. They might talk to the local Air Raid Precautions (**ARP**) warden, and then sneak off to hunt for souvenirs—parts of a bomb casing or, even better, parts of a shot-down German plane.

In the News

A famous American reporter named Edward R. Murrow was in Great Britain during the Blitz on London. His radio broadcasts told Americans what the Blitz was like: "Tonight, as on every other night, the rooftop watchers are peering out across the fantastic forest of London's chimney pots. The anti-aircraft gunners stand ready." Or, "It's a beautiful and lonesome city where men and women and children are trying to snatch a few hours sleep underground."

Sounds and smells of an air raid

- First, children heard air raid sirens wailing, then the drone of aircraft engines, the thump of bombs exploding, and crashes as buildings collapsed.

- Children also heard the "booming" of **anti-aircraft guns** firing at the bombers. Afterwards, they walked through rubble and puddles of water from fire-fighters' hoses, and smelled burning wood and explosive (from the bombs).

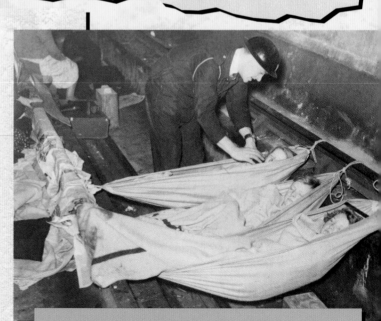

▲ In London, many people took shelter from air raids inside underground railway stations. In this photo, children are sleeping in hammocks slung between the rails!

◀ This young British girl has been rescued from a bombed house by a woman firefighter.

In the News

There were only two raids by a single aircraft on the mainland United States, and very few attacks by Japanese submarines. On February 23, 1942, a submarine shelled an oil facility near Santa Barbara, California. The next night enemy planes were reported above Los Angeles. There were no planes, but anti-aircraft gunners fired into the air and people rushed to their air raid shelters. The *Los Angeles Times* newspaper headlines wrongly declared "L.A Area Raided."

▼ People on both sides of the war suffered from the misery of air raids. This German woman is holding her baby in a crowded air raid shelter in Wehoff, Germany.

Lucky escape

There were many stories of lucky escapes from air raids. Some of them were amusing. In Scotland, a man was knocked to the ground by a bomb blast. Picking himself up, he saw what looked like a body, half-buried under rubble. The "body'" turned out to be a 14-year-old boy, unhurt but upset because his new pants had been blown off by the blast!

15

CHILDREN IN OCCUPIED EUROPE

In Europe, millions of children lived for five years under Nazi rule. They went to school, but grew up in an atmosphere of fear and hatred. In Germany, the Nazis believed children should be raised to become Nazis, too.

Life under enemy rule

Across Europe, the Nazi occupiers imposed strict laws. People had to stay inside after dark and they could not travel from one town to another without permission. Schools could teach only approved subjects that agreed with the Nazi view of history and the world. Children who looked "Aryan" (German) were encouraged to become Nazis, but others were persecuted simply because of their race or religion. A few **collaborators** helped the Germans, but most children in **occupied countries** grew to hate the invaders. They hated being cold and hungry, wearing worn-out clothes, and seeing cruelty everywhere.

Children in Germany

Hitler said, "German youth of the future must be as tough as leather and as hard as steel." German boys joined an organization called the *Jungvolk* (Young Folk) at the age of ten. When they were fourteen, they moved into the *Hitler Jugend* (Hitler Youth). Members of the Hitler Youth were taught Nazi ideas; they behaved like junior soldiers and paraded with flags. They were taught to obey Hitler and the Nazis, and trained through sports, camping, and hiking. Girls joined the *Bund Deutscher Mädel* (League of German Maidens, pictured here). They also exercised and were taught how to be a "good German wife and mother." So-called hooligans belonging to youth gangs were arrested by the police, and the gang leaders were executed.

April 9, 1940
German troops invade Norway. In Norway, Vidkun Quisling heads a government that supports Germany, but most Norwegians hate the Nazis.

June 30, 1940
German troops invade the Channel Islands, the only British territory to be occupied in the war.

June 22, 1941
Germany invades the Soviet Union. The Russians burn houses, machines, and crops as they retreat, so that the Germans cannot use them.

Resistance

Families in occupied countries secretly listened to radio broadcasts from the **Allies**. This is how they got news of the war, because the German government only broadcast **propaganda**. With help from the Allies, **Resistance** groups organized a secret war against the occupiers. Some brave children risked their lives to help the Resistance, such as by carrying messages and helping to hide Allied airmen who had been shot down.

Nazi atrocities

The Nazis acted with great cruelty. Children watched in horror as Jewish friends were taken away, never to be seen again. Thousands of children died in **concentration camps**. Others were murdered. In occupied countries the Nazis sometimes killed everyone in a village—including children—as a punishment for resistance attacks on German soldiers.

▲ Millions of Europeans suffered under Nazi occupation. These children are waiting for soup in occupied Prague, the capital of Czechoslovakia.

September 6, 1941	February–May 1942	July 1942
The Nazis order all Jews over the age of six to wear a yellow Star of David (to show they are Jews).	Japan conquers and occupies Malaya, Singapore, the Dutch East Indies, and the Philippines.	The Nazis begin sending Jews from Warsaw, the capital city of Poland, to death camps.

The Plight of Jewish Children

For Jewish children, the war held even worse terrors. The Nazis hunted down and exterminated (killed) as many Jews as they could in every occupied country. In Poland, the Nazis forced all the Jews of Warsaw (Poland's capital) to stay inside a walled district known as the **ghetto**. Inside the ghetto, people starved and got sick, and many died. Some people risked their lives to smuggle in food and medicine.

In July 1942, the Nazis began rounding up ghetto Jews and taking them away to death camps. For example, Mr. and Mrs. Goldsobel had been in the ghetto since October 1940, with their two daughters, Liliana and Sorela. In September 1942, the Goldsobel family was sent to a camp called Treblinka. There they were all killed in **gas chambers**. Sorela was only seven years old. The Goldsobel family had become four more victims of the **Holocaust**, the mass murder of roughly six million people during World War II.

Eyewitness

A young woman named Irena Sendler helped smuggle Jewish children out of the Warsaw ghetto. She hid them in potato sacks or in garbage carts—a mechanic carried one baby in his toolbox. "In my dreams I still hear the cries when they left their parents," she said later.

▲ Jewish children hold on to a trolley inside the Warsaw ghetto in Poland. Few of them would have survived the war—most were transported to death camps and then murdered. Others were killed in the Jewish uprising of 1943.

▶ Jewish children living under Nazi occupation were barred from playgrounds and sports arenas. They had to go to separate schools. All Jews, like this family, had to wear a star sewn on their clothes.

Children in Poland

- To make room for German settlers, the Nazis moved millions of Poles from western Poland.

- Many old people and children died on the journey east.

- Small children who looked "Aryan" were taken away and adopted by German families.

- In October 1940, all the Jews in Warsaw were forced into the ghetto.

▼ Of the three million Jews in Poland, most were arrested by the Nazis and taken by train to death camps such as Treblinka and Auschwitz. In these camps, men, women, and children were murdered with poison gas. The Polish Resistance tried to help Jews escape, but only 150,000 managed to survive by hiding.

GROWING UP AT WAR

Life for many children went on as usual—even if their school roof was blown off by a bomb. Children still went to school and played with their friends.

The routine of war

There was much less food to eat, and children got used to food **rationing**. They missed candy, and chocolate became a special treat. Governments gave advice about eating healthy meals with plenty of vegetables. The result was that some children were better fed and healthier than before the war. This was not the case in occupied countries. There, many children became thin and sick because of lack of food.

Millions of women went to work in the war industries. Many children returned from school to find their house empty and had to let themselves in. These "latchkey" children learned to care for younger brothers and sisters. Children also became used to air raids and drills. In Great Britain, people often read to pass the time in air raid shelters. Public libraries reported that children were borrowing more books.

In the News

In 1942 the first American soldiers arrived in Europe and Asia. Most foreign children only knew about the United States from movies. "We know a great deal about you ... most of the films we see are made in Hollywood," said a leaflet welcoming U.S. servicemen to Britain. U.S. troops were friendly. They often gave chocolate bars and chewing gum to children.

▶ Children playing on a bombsite. Bombed buildings were exciting but dangerous playgrounds—unexploded bombs often lay buried under the rubble. Some bombs were still being dug up in cities 60 years later!

1940-1941	October 13, 1940	1941
Heavy air raids on British cities destroy many children's homes.	Britain's Princess Elizabeth (age 14) broadcasts a radio message to child evacuees. Today she is Queen Elizabeth II.	Japanese schools abolish school holidays. Schoolchildren now have to help the war effort against China and, later, the United States.

▲ Members of the Hitler Youth formed part of the *Volkssturm*, a last-ditch "Home Guard" formed in 1944 to defend Germany from the Allies, who were advancing from east and west. Beginning in 1943, all German males over sixteen were called up for war work or military service.

Young people at war

Teenagers could remember what daily life was like before the war—when people could buy as much ice cream and chocolate as they could afford. Younger children had only hazy memories of a world without bombers, **blackouts**, and air raid drills. Teenagers knew that when they left school they would be involved in the war. Most would become war workers or servicemen and women. Some talked eagerly of becoming **Rangers** or fighter pilots. A few lied about their age and enlisted when they were as young as 13 or 14 years old. Thousands of the soldiers who landed in Normandy, France, on **D-Day** in 1944 had been at school when the war began.

21

1942
Rationing begins in the United States. By 1943, goods such as meat, sugar, coffee, rubber, tires, and gasoline are rationed.

1943
Thousands of young Americans become Victory Farm Volunteers and help on farms.

1944
Young Germans are forced to join the *Volkssturm*, a home guard to defend Germany against invasion.

Wartime Toys and Games

GROWING UP AT WAR

There were fewer toys in wartime because most toys had been made in Germany or Japan. In America, toy factories had to start making war materials. There was not any spare metal to make toys. A few companies made wooden cars and trucks from spare wood.

Children still had fun with homemade toys, such as knitted dolls or wooden airplanes. Many toys had a war theme. Small children colored in coloring books with pictures of soldiers, sailors, and airmen. They could also dress paper dolls in many different uniforms using special kits. Other popular toys with a war theme included model planes, toy tanks, battleships for the bathtub, and toy soldiers.

For quieter moments, there were card games, board games (such as Chutes and Ladders), dominoes, marbles, and jigsaw puzzles. Hitler made a good joke-target for dart board games: kids used Hitler's open mouth as the bull's-eye!

▲ Children enjoyed dressing up. The most popular games used characters like soldiers, sailors, pilots, and nurses.

AIRCRAFT OF THE R.A.F.
Some Famous Types - I.

◄ "Spot the plane" books printed pictures of planes, so that children could tell whether a plane was "one of ours" or "one of theirs." Similar silhouettes appeared on aircraft identification posters in factories and military bases, so the books made children feel grown-up.

▶ Traditional toys were expensive. Toymakers had to find new materials, since rubber, cork, and rope were scarce. These U.S. children are playing with models made of paper instead of wood, which was needed for the war effort.

Toys for the military

A toy called a View-Master was used by the American armed forces! The viewer has special pictures that can be seen in three dimensions. The armed forces used the viewers for training to show what enemy ships and planes looked like.

In the News

"A girl's wartime adventure on a lonely Pacific island" was the title for a typical story in wartime children's magazines. One magazine showed two girls confronting Japanese soldiers, with the dramatic caption: "ALONE AGAINST THE INVADERS." Readers never doubted that the girls would win.

Eyewitnesses

"Once I was given a soldier uniform kit. It had a helmet and a cardboard front of uniform ... and I had a wooden dagger and a belt to go with it. I recall saluting a soldier once and he saluted back."

A German schoolboy, who was six years old when the war began.

"We never had much money ... I thought that we were rich. Most kids didn't have horses. And we had sleds and bicycles and ice skates and that kind of thing."

Wilma Briggs, who lived on a farm in East Greenwich, Rhode Island.

FAMILY LIFE

FAMILY LIFE

Family life in wartime was different. Mothers went to work. Fathers were often away for months. Even when the fighting stopped and peace returned, becoming a family again wasn't always easy.

Many families were split up because men (fathers, brothers, and uncles) were away fighting or doing war work. Mothers were often away at work also—many more women worked full-time than before the war. Older sisters left home to join the services or to add their skills to the war effort.

Some evacuee children were away from home for years. So were fathers, particularly those held captive as **prisoners of war**. Many were killed in action and did not return at all. Some marriages broke up under the strain of wartime separation. Divorce, fairly rare before the war, became more common.

Children on their own

The war made many children mature (grow up) more quickly. They had to do many household jobs and chores that their parents had done. Some grew up without one or both parents. Others lost brothers and sisters who were killed in battle. When servicemen came home in 1945, small children often did not recognize the man who said he was their father.

▶ Children did their part to help with domestic chores such as washing floors. In the 1940s, it was quite common for parents to send children to stores to buy food and other items.

1940
The Walt Disney films *Pinocchio* and *Fantasia* are the favorite movies of the year for children.

October 1940
The United States calls up men for military service. Thousands, later millions, of men leave home.

1942
Families are told to grow more food during the "Dig for Victory" campaign.

Having fun as a family

At home, families listened to the radio in the evenings. Children had their own radio programs and also enjoyed comedy shows and music. Most children also looked forward to a trip to the movie theater, which cost about ten cents. There they saw news of the war as well as the movies.

People tried to enjoy holidays and birthdays even if they could not buy fancy decorations or frosted cakes. Few families had cars, and gasoline was rationed, so trips had to be by foot, bike, bus, or train. In many occupied countries and Britain it was difficult to visit the beach, because there were soldiers, explosive mines, and barbed-wire defenses against enemy invasion.

▲ Parties were fun, but mothers found it hard to get enough sugar and fruit to make birthday cakes! Birthday cards were also smaller during the war because paper was rationed.

1942

Fuel rationing means that it is difficult for families to use their cars for trips.

July 1943

More than 125,000 pre-school children regularly spend the day in childcare centers while their mothers are at work.

1943

Lassie Come Home, a movie about a dog that rescues its master, is a favorite with families.

Together Again?

In 1945, people celebrated the end of the war with parades and parties. Millions of men started to come home, and families were reunited. It was a strange time for many children who had grown up during the war. Some were scared of their "strange" fathers, who they had not seen for many years.

Victory meant peace, but the war had caused misery for millions of people in the world. In Germany and Japan, there were no victory celebrations. In those defeated countries, families had been shattered, like their bombed cities. In homes from Moscow to Chicago, many families mourned the loss of someone they had loved. The world was also learning the horror of the Holocaust in which six million Jews and other people, many of them children, had been murdered.

Across Asia and Europe, millions of people were homeless. Thousands of families had been separated. Organizations such as the Red Cross worked to reunite parents and children.

▶ Children in Europe got used to seeing foreign soldiers, like this American GI. Men and women from all over the world, and in many uniforms, served in countries away from their homes.

Countdown to victory

- The Allies invaded France in June 1944. By the winter, they were in Germany.

- The Soviet armies invaded Germany from the east.

- By May 1945, the war in Europe was over.

- In the Pacific, U.S. forces led the Allied advance on Japan, island by island.

- The dropping of two atomic bombs on Japan ended the Pacific war in August 1945.

FAMILY LIFE

▶ A U.S. Navy officer arrives home at the end of the war. Reuniting with family after years of separation was not always easy.

Eyewitness

Jean Barr was twelve years old when Pearl Harbor was attacked in 1941. She remembers the end of the war: "I vividly recall my Uncle Ed's homecoming. The whole family gathered on the large front porch, anticipating his arrival. Ed appeared walking, then running up the porch steps. He and his father embraced for several minutes. We all took a turn for a hug. Tears of joy and relief were all around us."

Letters and telegrams

"It is with regret that I am writing to confirm the recent telegram informing you of the death of your son ... who was killed in action ... I know the sorrow this message has brought you and it is my hope that ... the knowledge of his heroic service to his country may be of comfort to you."

This is part of a government letter. Mothers and wives dreaded official telegrams and letters that told them their loved ones had been killed in the war.

◀ Special camps were set up for Europe's millions of displaced people—people who had lost homes and families. The continent had become like a huge refugee camp. Among the homeless were many children who had been separated from their parents.

27

PEACE RETURNS

In 1945, the war ended. In May, people in Europe celebrated VE, or Victory in Europe, day. Then, in August, the whole world celebrated Victory over Japan day.

When they heard the news, people flocked into the streets. There was shouting and laughing, cheering and crying. Soon children were treated to parties, and there were parades, music, and dancing. A nine-year-old British girl later wrote how exciting it was, saying: "I had never seen a street-lamp working or a shop window lit up." There would be candy again!

After the parties

Then the parties were over, and people went back to work. Schools reopened for the new year. Many children had grown up with war, with its sounds and smells, excitements and fears. Going back to school seemed almost dull.

In September 1945 the new president, Harry S Truman, said: "We think of all the men and women and children who during these years have carried on at home, in lonesomeness and anxiety and fear." He knew that children had played their part in winning the war.

▶ These children in London are making the most of their VE Day celebration party. Peace at last! The younger children would not have been able to remember what daily life was like before the war.

TIMELINE

1939

August 30 16,000 children are evacuated from Paris, France.

September 1 Germany invades Poland. World War II begins.

September 3 France and Britain declare war on Germany. Evacuation of children from Britain's cities begins.

1940

January People in Britain start to get used to food rationing.

April Germany invades Denmark and Norway.

May German armies invade Belgium, the Netherlands, and France. Many children are among the fleeing refugees.

May British boys age seventeen can join the new Local Defense Volunteers, the Home Guard, to help the army protect Britain.

May–June A British army is evacuated from Dunkirk, in France.

June France surrenders. The U.S. government tells all foreigners they must register with the Federal authorities because it is believed that they might be a threat to security.

July–September Children in southern England watch planes "dog-fighting" overhead during the Battle of Britain.

September London children experience their first bombs: the Blitz on London begins.

1941

March The British government sets up many nurseries for babies and very young children so that women can work in factories.

April Germany invades Greece and Yugoslavia.

June 22 Germany invades the Soviet Union.

June Clothes rationing begins in Britain.

December 7 Japanese attack on Pearl Harbor brings the United States into the war.

1942

February Singapore and the Philippines fall to Japan, which also bombs northern Australia.

March U.S. government begins to intern (put) more than 120,000 Japanese-Americans in special camps because it thinks they may not be loyal to the United States.

May Start of some gasoline rationing in the United States.

June The last Jewish schools in Germany are closed by the Nazis.

July Candy is rationed in Britain.

October The U.S. government freezes wages, rents, and prices.

December The British government plans to offer school dinners to all children.

1943

February The Allies begin bombing Germany night and day. A German army surrenders at Stalingrad, marking the end of German advance eastwards into the Soviet Union.

April-May Many foods are now rationed in the United States.

May All women between the ages of 18 and 45 in Britain must do at least part-time war work.

July Allies land in Sicily to begin the invasion of Italy.

1944

March Heavy bombing raids on Berlin, the German capital city.

June 6 D-Day; Allied armies invade France.

June 12/13 First German V-1 flying bomb falls on London. New evacuation plan is put into action to remove children from danger.

August 25 Children join the celebrations as the French capital, Paris, is liberated by the Allies.

September 8 The first V-2 rocket falls on London.

September Allied armies enter Germany. The Nazis form a Home Guard of people age 16 to 60.

October German bread ration is cut to one loaf a week. American forces win the naval and air battle of Leyte Gulf, in the Philippines.

December The Battle of the Bulge begins. German army attacks on American forces kill many soldiers.

1945

April U.S. troops land on Okinawa, close to the Japanese mainland.

April 30 Hitler kills himself as Soviet armies close in on Berlin.

May 7 Germany surrenders.

May 8 VE Day is a day of parades and parties across Britain as children join in the peace celebrations.

August 6 The Allies drop an atomic bomb on Hiroshima and another on Nagasaki three days later. The war is soon over.

August 14 People celebrate V-J (Victory over Japan) Day.

GLOSSARY

air raid attack by aircraft dropping bombs on cities

air raid shelter building designed to protect people inside from bombs

Allies nations that fought against Japan, Germany, and Italy during World War II

ancestry a person's family background

anti-aircraft guns big guns firing shells thousands of yards into the air to hit or scare off enemy planes

ARP stands for Air Raid Precautions, later changed to Civil Defense. An organization in Britain that dealt with bombs and bomb damage.

Battle of Britain air battle between the Royal Air Force and the German air force or *Luftwaffe* in 1940

blackout measures to reduce all lights showing at night in order to hide possible targets from enemy bombers

Blitz short for *Blitzkrieg*, German for "lightning war." The term is used to describe the German bombing attack on Britain, beginning in 1940.

civil war fighting between people who live in the same country

civilian person not in the armed forces

collaborators people who help an enemy invader of their country

concentration camp prison in which Jews and other prisoners of the Nazis were kept in terrible conditions

D-Day name for the Allied invasion of France, on June 6, 1944

evacuation act of moving people from dangerous to safer places

evacuees people who were evacuated

gas chamber room in which people were killed by poison gas

ghetto sealed area of a town in which Jews were forced to live

Holocaust Nazi mass murder of Jews and other peoples during World War II

Jews followers of the religion of Judaism

Nazi member of the National Socialist German Workers' Party, led by Adolf Hitler

occupied countries countries invaded and ruled by an enemy during wartime

persecution deliberate cruel treatment

prisoner of war person captured by the enemy during a war

propaganda control of information to show your own side in a good light and the enemy in a bad way

Ranger American soldier trained for raiding missions

rationing controlling the supply of food and other goods. People were given ration books with coupons to use when buying rationed goods.

refugees people forced to leave their homes because of natural disaster, famine, persecution, or war

Resistance groups of people in occupied countries who worked and fought against the enemy

siren a machine used to sound the alarm when enemy bombing planes were approaching

FINDING OUT MORE

If you are interested in finding out more about World War II, here are some more books you might find useful.

Further reading

Your local public library's adult section should have plenty of war books, including books about what it was like to live as a child during wartime. Written by people who were actually there, such books will give you an idea of what ordinary people thought about the war and their part in it.

Books for younger readers

Adams, Simon. *World War II.* New York: DK Children, 2004.

Ambrose, Stephen E. *The Good Fight.* New York: Simon & Schuster, 2001.

Colman, Penny. *Rosie the Riveter: Women Working on the Homefront in World War II.* New York: Knopf, 1995.

Dolan, Edward F. *America in WWII – 1943.* Brookfield: Millbrook, 1992.

Josephson, Judith Pinkerton. *Growing Up in World War II: 1941–1945.* Minneapolis: Lerner, 2002.

King, David C. *World War II Days.* New York: Wiley, 2000.

Panchyk, Richard. *WWII for Kids.* Chicago: Chicago Review Press, 2002.

Tanaka, Shelley. *Attack on Pearl Harbor.* New York: Hyperion, 2001.

Also the Heinemann Library *Holocaust* and *Witness to History* series (several titles).

INDEX